Portrush Financial
Lifeboat Station

90 Minute Wealth Building Breakthrough Session Workbook

125 Rickey Blvd #866
Bear DE 19701-0866
(302)669-9156

Portrush Financial
Lifeboat Station

Hello Prosperous One!

Congratulations on taking this wonderful step to your prosperous life. My name is Sandra Frisbey and I am your Wealth Coach. As your Wealth Coach, I will instruct you and guide you in ways and techniques that will rescue you from detrimental practices that have kept you from living your most prosperous life.

I know what it is like to get paid and find out that there is nothing left for you. To feel as though there has got to be more to life than working and paying bills. That was the moment I decided to get out of debt and get control of my finances! Once I was able to get control of my debt and finances, a different world opened up for me. I was able to buy the car I desired, renovate my house, contribute to my son's college and send my other son to private school.

The techniques that I am instructing you in this workbook are the same techniques I used to accomplish my freedom from debt and financial disaster. If you truly desire freedom and control over your finances, this session is for you. I won't lie to you. It will take discipline and focus, but you have all that and I am going to show you how to tap into it.

Today, your life has changed. You are no longer running after money, but money is running after you! It just needs to be shown where to go. This session is designed to do just that!

Congratulations again! Persevere, you win!

God Bless,

Miss Sandra
Wealth Coach
Portrush Financial Lifeboat Station
portrushflb@gmail.com
(302)669-9156

Portrush Financial
Lifeboat Station

Common Questions Asked About Credit

By Diana Bernal posted 1/29/11
www.portrushflbstation.blogspot.com

Whoever is wise will observe these things, And they will understand the lovingkindness of the Lord. Psalm 107:43 (NKJV)

Q. How do I build good credit?
A. Pay all bills on time and use only about 30% of available credit.

Q. How do I get my free credit report annually?
A. Under the Fair and Accurate Credit Reporting Act go
to http://www.annualcreditreport.com/.

Q. How can I get my free credit score?
A. http://www.creditkarma.com/ (You will need an e-mail address).

Q. What is a FICO score?
A. The FICO Score (300-850) is created by Fair, Isaac and company to determine your credit risk.

Q. How is my credit compiled?
A. 35% on your payment history, 30% on amount already owed, 15% on length of credit history, 10% on new credit, 10% on type of credit.

Q. Should I pay my credit card bills in full each month?
A. Yes. If you cannot pay the bill in full, please pay at least more than the minimum. Don't pay just the minimum. Read your bill carefully. It tells you what happens if you pay the minimum.

Q. Where can I get some help with debt reduction planning?
A. Visit http://cgi.money.cnn.com/tools/debtplanner/debtplanner.jsp for help with planning.

Q. How do I reach my Credit Bureaus?
A. Experian 888-397.3742, Equifax 800-685-1111, Trans Union 800-916-8800.

Q. What reports should I order annually?
A. Get credit reports annually at http://www.annualcreditreport.com/ or 1-877-322-8228; Employment Background Check/Homeowers and Auto Insurance Claims

at http://www.choicetrust.com/ or 1-866-312-8076; MIB-Consumer's Medical Condition at http://www.mib.com/html/request_your_record.html or 1-866-692-6901; Unlawful Detainer Registry (residential/tenant history) at http://www.choicetrust.com/ or 1-877-448-5732; ChexSystems at http://www.consumerdebit.com/ or 1800-428-9623.

Q. How long does bad credit remain on my credit account?
A. Civil Judgement - 7 years; Unpaid tax liens - Indefinite; Other derogatory - 7 years; Paid tax liens - 7 years from date paid; Chapter 7 bankruptcy - 11-10 years; Chapter 13 bankruptcy - 10-13 years; Chapter 13 dismissal/discharges - 7 years; Bankruptcies voluntarily dismissed - 7 years.

Q. When may someone look at my entire un-purged credit history?
A. If you are applying for credit over $150,000, Insurance over $150,000 or for a job more than $75,000/year.

Q. How do I correct errors on my credit report?
A. Write and send documentation (duplicates not originals). If bureau made mistake, it must correct it; notify all other credit bureaus; notify those who looked at credit report in the past 6 months - REQUEST IT! Bureau has 30 days to reply and send corrected credit report.

Q. If I am a victim of Identify Theft, what should I do?
A. File a police report with the Financial Crimes Unit.

- Contact the fraud departments and have a fraud alert placed on your credit file: Equifax - 1-800-525-6285; Experian - 1-888-397-3742; TransUnion - 1-800-680-7289
- Other Credit Reports: Equifax - 1-800-685-1111; Experian - 1-888-397-3742; TransUnion - 1-800-916-8800
- Open new accounts etc. Insist on password only access to your account.
- Contact/Inform the following: SSA (Social Security Admin); FTC (Federal Trade Commission); IRS (Internal Revenue Service) and DMV (Division of Motor Vehicles)

Q. Can you tell me the different consumer bankruptcies available to me?
A. Chapter 7 = liquidation -- No debts to repay or Chapter 13 = reorganization -- Sort of debt consolidation where you keep assets.

Personal Notes

_____
_____
_____
_____
_____
_____
_____
_____
_____
_____
_____
_____
_____
_____
_____
_____
_____
_____
_____
_____
_____
_____
_____
_____
_____
_____
_____
_____
_____

**Portrush Financial
Lifeboat Station**

Debt Reduction Plan

Tips for Having a Successful Reduction Plan:

- Know how much you owe don't guess. Get an official credit report. You can get a free report from http://annualcreditreport.com. You can also get your credit score for a small fee or go to http://creditkarma.com for your free credit score.
- Consider paying off any judgments or accounts that are in collection first. They have the greatest impact on your credit.
- Start with the lowest amount when choosing the debt to paid off. This will encourage you to continue paying off your debts when you see how easily it was to pay off the first.
- When choosing a payment amount, choose an amount that is significant but not stressful. You don't want to choose amount that will be hard to keep or amount that will stretch out the payments for a long period of time. The purpose is to pay off your debt in the shortest amount of time without over stressing yourself.
- If possible keep the number of payments to 12 or less.

1. **List your debt.**

   Lender   Amount owed

   _____ $_____.___

   _____   _____.___

   _____   _____.___

   _____   _____.___

   _____   _____.___

   _____   _____.___

   _____   _____.___

   _____   _____.___

   _____   _____.___

   _____   _____.___

   Total Owed $_____.___

2. **List largest amount owed to the smallest amount owed.**

$_____.___

_____.___

_____.___

_____.___

_____.___

_____.___

_____.___

_____.___

_____.___

_____.___

3. **Chose the debt you desire to pay off.**

Lender _____   Amount _____

4. **Commitment Statement.**

"I (we) can pay off this debt with _____ payments of $_____. "

5. **Payoff Schedule**

No.	Date of Scheduled Payment	Amt. of Payment	Balance
			Beg. Bal.
1.			
2.			
3			
4.			
5.			
6.			
7.			
8.			
9.			
10.			
11.			
12.			

Personal Notes

"*Money is only a tool. It will take you wherever you wish, but it will not replace you as the driver.*"
— *Ayn Rand, Atlas Shrugged*

PERSONAL BUDGET

PAY DATE: _____

INCOME: SAVINGS ACCT BAL $ _____

PAY CHECK: $_____
OTHER INCOME: $ _____   **Pay 1**
OTHER INCOME: $ _____

TOTAL INCOME: $ _____

EXPENSES	$ AMT BUDGETED	DATE PAID	$ ACTUAL PAYMENT
MORTGAGE / RENT			
2ND MORTGAGE			
SAVINGS			
RETIREMENT			
GIVING/TITHES/OFFERINGS			
ELECTRIC/GAS/OIL			
CABLE/INTERNET/PHONE			
CELL PHONE			
CAR LOAN			
CAR INSURANCE			
STUDENT LOAN			
PERSONAL LOAN			
CREDIT CARD ( )			
CREDIT CARD ( )			
GAS / TOLLS			
LIFE INSURANCE			
TRASH			
WATER			
ASSOCIATION DUES			
FOOD			
ENTERTAINMENT			
CLOTHING			
OTHER ( )			
TOTAL EXPENSES			

Portrush Financial
Lifeboat Station

SAVINGS ACCOUNT BALANCE

Pay 1

BEGINNING BALANCE $_____

DEPOSIT $_____   REASON _____

DEPOSIT $_____   REASON _____

WITHDRAWAL $_____   REASON _____

WITHDRAWAL $_____   REASON _____

ENDING BALANCE $_____

@Melissa King/Dreamstine Stock Photos

Portrush Financial Lifeboat Station

DISCRETIONARY INCOME

PAY DATE:

(Pay 1)

TOTAL INCOME: $_____

MINUS

TOTAL EXPENSES: $_____

EQUALS

DISCRETIONARY
INCOME: $_____

DISCRETIONARY INCOME SPENDING

DATE	DESCRIPTION	$ AMOUNT SPENT

PERSONAL BUDGET

PAY DATE: _____

INCOME: **SAVINGS ACCT BAL $** _____

PAY CHECK: $_____
OTHER INCOME: $ _____   **Pay 2**
OTHER INCOME: $ _____

TOTAL INCOME: $ _____

EXPENSES	$ AMT BUDGETED	DATE PAID	$ ACTUAL PAYMENT
MORTGAGE / RENT			
2ND MORTGAGE			
SAVINGS			
RETIREMENT			
GIVING/TITHES/OFFERINGS			
ELECTRIC/GAS			
CABLE/INTERNET/PHONE			
CELL PHONE			
CAR LOAN			
CAR INSURANCE			
STUDENT LOAN			
PERSONAL LOAN			
CREDIT CARD ( )			
CREDIT CARD ( )			
GAS / TOLLS			
LIFE INSURANCE			
TRASH			
WATER			
ASSOCIATION DUES			
FOOD			
ENTERTAINMENT			
CLOTHING			
OTHER ( )			
TOTAL EXPENSES			

SAVINGS ACCOUNT BALANCE

Pay 2

BEGINNING BALANCE $_____

DEPOSIT $_____   REASON _____

DEPOSIT $_____   REASON _____

WITHDRAWAL $_____   REASON _____

WITHDRAWAL $_____   REASON _____

ENDING BALANCE $_____

@Melissa King/Dreamstime Stock Photos

Portrush Financial Lifeboat Station

DISCRETIONARY INCOME

PAY DATE:

(Pay 2)

TOTAL INCOME: $_____

MINUS

TOTAL EXPENSES: $_____

EQUALS

DISCRETIONARY
INCOME: $_____

DISCRETIONARY INCOME SPENDING

DATE	DESCRIPTION	$ AMOUNT SPENT

Portrush Financial
Lifeboat Station

Personal Notes

THE CYCLE OF MONEY

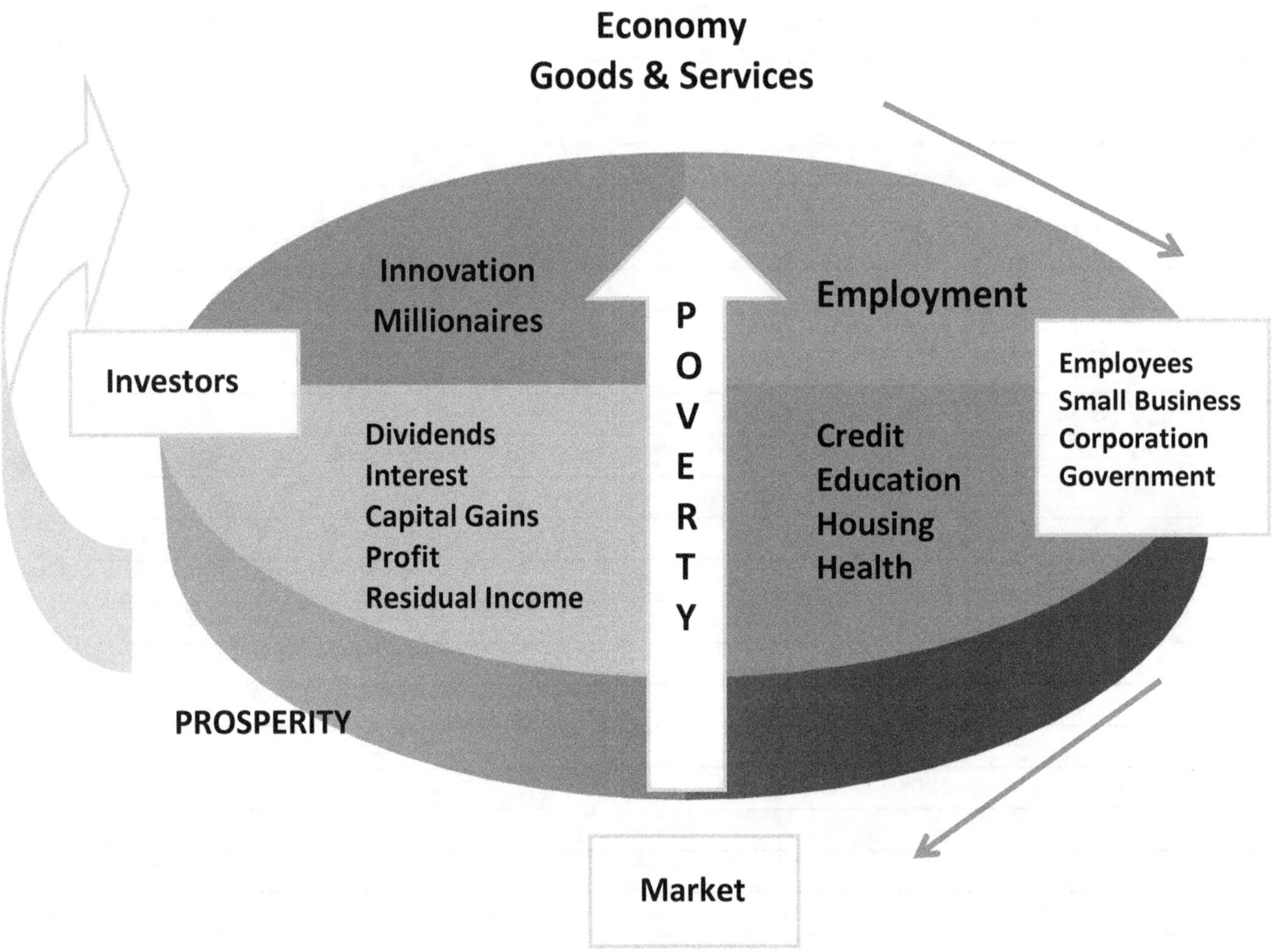

**Economy
Goods & Services**

Innovation
Millionaires

Employment

Investors

**P
O
V
E
R
T
Y**

Dividends
Interest
Capital Gains
Profit
Residual Income

Credit
Education
Housing
Health

Employees
Small Business
Corporation
Government

PROSPERITY

Market

Portrush Financial
Lifeboat Station

SEVEN FIELDS OF PROSPERITY™
WORKSHEET

Directions:
Listed below are the seven fields that contain your ability to produce wealth. Under each field you will find 10 areas of production. Check off each area that is producing wealth in your life today. To the right of each field is a box for you to write the total number of areas checked off for that field.

THE FINANCIAL FIELD

__ Checking Acct
__ Savings Acct
__ Retirement Acct
__ Life Insurance
__ Credit Score 750 or above

__ Wages /Retirement Income
__ Investments (Stocks, bonds, mutual Funds)
__ Will
__ Emergency Acct (3X MONTHLY INCOME)
__ College Fund/Trust Acct

Total Checked

THE REAL ESTATE FIELD

__ Rent/Own home
__ Pay Rent/ Mortgage on time
__ Friendly with neighbors
__ Real Estate Investments
__ 15 yr or less Mortgage

__ Home improvement made within 2 yrs
__ Pay utility bills on time
__ Obey rules of community
__ Pay taxes
__ Know assessed value of home

Total Checked

THE EDUCATION FIELD

__ Diploma/GED
__ Masters Degree
__ Read 1 book per month
__ Subscribe to blog or magazine
__ Learned a new skill this yr

__ Bachelor Science/Arts Degree
__ Doctors Degree
__ Have a Mentors
__ Took extended Educ. Classes within 2 yrs
__ Tudor/train /mentor

Total Checked

THE HEALTH FIELD

__ Health Insurance
__ Long Term Insurance
__ Dentist
__ Exercise
__ BMI under 30

__ Disability Insurance/Sick leave
__ Primary Doctor
__ Eye Doctor
__ Vitamins/Supplements
__ Yearly examinations

Total Checked

THE COMMUNITY FIELD

Total Checked

__ Attend Community meetings
__ Coach or lead youth group
__ Volunteer
__ Donate Blood
__ Vote

__ Participate in PTA/Auxillary Group
__ Hold office of authority in Community
__ Donate money
__ Sponsor a community event
__ Participate in a neighborhood watch

THE BALANCE AND HARMONY FIELD

Total Checked

__ Vacation once a year
__ Saving 10% of income
__ Attend family functions
__ Support your children
__ Respect your neighbor

__ Honor your commitments
__ Work 50 hours or less a week
__ Honor your parents
__ Avoid strife and disagreements
__ Payments (mortgage, credit cards, loans) less than 36% of monthly income.

THE WORSHIP FIELD

Total Checked

__ Attend Church regularly
__ Give regular offerings
__ Prayer life
__ Forgiveness of others
__ Fellowship outside of church

__ Pay tithes
__ Serve in church (usher, altar, choir etc)
__ Read Bible daily
__ Attend or Attended Bible School
__ Regularly testify of God's Love

Wealth Producer Percentage

Directions: Add up the total boxes for all of the fields and place the total in the box provided (as the dividend) under the Total Wealth Score label. Then divide that number by 70, multiply that result by 100 to get your wealth percentage. Your total wealth percentage identifies where you are as a wealth producer while your individual totals define your wealth in each field.

Total Wealth Score   Wealth Percentage

$$\frac{}{70} \times 100 \qquad \%$$

@Piotr Majka/Dreamstime Stock Photos

Portrush Financial Lifeboat Station

Wealth Building Worksheet

Directions: For each field listed below identify an area of production (goal) that you are missing or in need of improvement. For each goal there is space for you to create a strategy for obtaining that goal. Your strategy will consist of ten (10) tasks. Each task builds on each other. For example task #2 cannot be accomplished without doing task #1 first; task #3 cannot be accomplished without doing tasks #1 & 2 and so on.

Finance Goal: _____

1. _____
2. _____
3. _____
4. _____
5. _____
6. _____
7. _____
8. _____
9. _____
10. _____

Real Estate Goal: _____

1. _____
2. _____
3. _____
4. _____
5. _____
6. _____
7. _____
8. _____
9. _____
10. _____

Education Goal: _____

1. _____
2. _____
3. _____
4. _____
5. _____
6. _____
7. _____
8. _____
9. _____
10. _____

Health Goal: _____

1. _____
2. _____
3. _____
4. _____
5. _____
6. _____
7. _____
8. _____
9. _____
10. _____

Community Goal: _____

1. _____
2. _____
3. _____
4. _____
5. _____
6. _____
7. _____
8. _____
9. _____
10. _____

Balance/Harmony Goal: _____

    1. _____
    2. _____
    3. _____
    4. _____
    5. _____
    6. _____
    7. _____
    8. _____
    9. _____
   10. _____

Worship Goal: _____

    1. _____
    2. _____
    3. _____
    4. _____
    5. _____
    6. _____
    7. _____
    8. _____
    9. _____
   10. _____

@Mark Bolton/Dreamstime Stock Photos

Personal Notes

_____
_____
_____
_____
_____
_____
_____
_____
_____
_____
_____
_____
_____
_____
_____
_____
_____
_____
_____
_____
_____
_____
_____
_____
_____
_____
_____
_____
_____
_____
_____
_____
_____
_____

FINANCIAL DEFINITIONS

In order for you to build wealth you must understand the language in which wealth operates. Having command of the language which governs wealth will give you understanding. With understanding comes authority. Below you will find definitions that pertain to wealth. Read out loud each word and its definition. Do this daily until you have full comprehension. Note: There are many more words you will need to know to become a master of the language. This exercise will help you as you enter into the world of finance and wealth. Once you have learned this list, make it a daily habit to add a new wealth definition to your vocabulary. (Note: All Definitions were obtained from Investopedia. For more information please visit: http://www.investopedia.com)

Wisdom is the principal thing; Therefore get wisdom. And in all your getting, get understanding.
Proverbs 4:7 NKJV

Accrue - To accumulate periodically over time.

Adverse Action – Denial of credit, employment, insurance or other benefits.

Annuity – A financial product that is designed to accept and grow funds until a certain time when the funds are paid out through a stream of payments.

Appraisal – An estimated valuation of property.

Attrition – Natural reduction of staff and employees through retirement and resignation.

Bear Market – When prices in the market are falling.

Blue-Chip Stock- Stock of a large, well established and financially sound company.

Broker – An individual who provides investment services for a fee.

Budget – A snapshot of revenue and expenses over a specified period of time.

Bull Market – When prices in a market are rising.

Capital Gain – The increase between the purchase price and the sold price.

Capitalism – An economic system that is based on private ownership and the production of goods and services for profit.

Cash Advance – Cash given by credit card companies at a high interest rate.

Compound Interest – Interest that is calculated on the initial principal and then calculated on the accumulated interest.

Cosign – To sign and obligate yourself to another person's debt.

Credit Score – An numeric expression of a person's creditworthiness.

Debt Consolidation – The act of simplifying your debt by combining several loans or debts into one loan.

Deflation – A decline in prices due to a reduction of money or credit being injected into the economy. The value of a dollar increases and the price of products decrease.

Discretionary Income - The amount left for spending, investing or saving.

Diversification - A technique that mixes a wide variety of investments within a portfolio to lower risk.

Dividend - A distribution of a portion of a company's earnings.

Earned Income – Wages, salary, tips, commissions and bonuses derived from active participation in a trade or business.

Economy - Everything related to the production and consumption of goods and services.

Emergency Fund – Set aside funds to be used in an emergency.

Equity – Ownership in asset.

Escrow – Funds or assets that are held by a third party until certain conditions are met.

Exercise – To put into effect the right specified in a contract such as the right to buy or sell in options trading.

Federal Credit Union – FCU – A bank organized under federal credit union regulations instead of state banking laws. It operates like a retail bank except members are partial owners.

Federal Housing Administration – FHA- A government mortgage insurance agency that protects lenders from losses associated with mortgage default.

Flexible Spending Account – FSA – A savings account set that allows employees to set aside a portion on their earnings to pay for qualified expenses.

Futures – An obligation to purchase an asset at a future price on a predetermined date.

Garnishment – A hold on money or property by a third party to pay a debt to a creditor.

Goodwill – An intangible asset such as the value of company's brand name, solid customer base, good customer relations, good employee relations and any patents or technology.

Grace Period – A period that allows payments to be received after the due date without a penalty.

Gross Income – Total income before taxes or deductions.

Gross National Product – GNP – The total national output of goods and services for a country.

Hard Inquiry – A credit report inquiry when an individual applies for credit such as a mortgage, credit card or auto loan.

Home Equity – Current market value of a home or property less any remaining mortgage payments.

Home Inspection –A qualified assessment of a real estate property's condition.

Imputed Cost – The cost you would have earned if you invested an asset instead of using it.

Index Fund – A mutual fund that is set up to match or track the components of a market index, such as the Standard & Poor 500 index (S&P 500).

Individual Retirement Account – IRA – An investment account that allows an individual to earn funds for retirement.

Inflation – A rise in prices and a decrease in purchasing power.

Initial Public Offering – IPO - The first sale of stock by a private company to the public, generally to expand capital.

Joint Account – An account shared by two or more individuals that have access to the funds.
Judgment – A court order to pay a specified sum of money arising from a lawsuit.

Last Will And Testament - A legal communication of a person's final wishes, as pertaining to possessions and dependents.

Lease - A legal document outlining the terms and conditions of the rental of property between two parties.

Lemon Laws – Regulations to protect individuals when they purchase a vehicle that is defect in use, safety or value.

Lien – The legal right of a creditor to sell collateral property when a debtor fails to pay a debt.

Limited Liability – Liability that is limited to the amount invested.

Living Will – A legal communication of an individual's wishes if incapacitation occurs.

Margin - Money borrowed to purchase securities.

Marital Deduction – A tax deduction that transfers assets tax free to an individual's spouse in the event of death.

Mid Cap - A company with a market capitalization between $2 and $10 billion.

Money Market Account – An account that pays a higher interest rate than a savings account.

Moody's – A research company that rates fixed income securities such as bonds.

Mortgage Interest – Interest charged on a loan where a residence is used as security.
Mortgage Short Sale – The sale of property for less than the outstanding mortgage balance.

Mutual Fund – A pool of funds collected from many individuals to invest in securities.

No-Load Fund - A mutual fund where there is no fee or commission for the selling or buying of shares.

Nominal –A rate that does not adjust for inflation or market fluctuations.

Notary – An official witness who verifies an individual's signature. Also known as a 'notary public'.

Offering – Sale of a security by a company.

Option – A financial by-product (a contractual right) sold by one party to another party.

Ordinary Dividends – A share of a company's profits paid out to shareholders and taxed as ordinary income.

Origination Fee - An up-front fee charged by a lender for processing a new loan application.

Origination Points – A fee charged by lenders for processing and approving mortgage loans.

Par Value – A bond's face value.

Passive Activity – Any activity where the taxpayer did not materially participate.

Passive Income – Income derived from activity in which the taxpayer did not participate.

Pell Grant - Federal financial aid grant based on need and does not require repayment.

PLUS Loan - A low-cost loan offered to parents of students currently enrolled in post-secondary education.

Prime Rate – An interest rate given by banks to customers who are considered credit worthy, usually large corporations. This rate is usually lower than the rate charged to other customers.

Probate – The legal process to determine the validity of a will.

Profit and Loss Statement - P&L - A financial summary of revenues, costs and expenses incurred during a specific period of time.

Quantitative Easing – A Federal Reserve policy to purchase government securities or other securities from the market to lower interest rates and increase money supply.

Recession – A significant decline in production, employment, income and trade that lasts over two consecutive quarters.

Recession Proof – A term used to describe an asset that can withstand a recession such as gold or gold stocks.

Refinance – Revision of a loan with new payments and terms.

Rescission – A court order repeal of a contract.

Residual Income – Income that is left after all personal debts have been paid.

Roth IRA – An individual retirement plan where the contributions are not tax deductible and qualified distributions are tax free.

Rule Of 72 – A rule that computes the number of years required to double your money by dividing the compound return into 72. Example: A savings account paying 12% interest will double in six years (72÷12=6),

Secured Note - A type of loan that is backed by the borrower's assets.

Seed Capital – Capital used to start a business.

Series EE Bond – U. S. government savings bond that is sold at a discount and pays interest at maturity.

Signing Bonus – A financial award offered to an individual as an incentive for joining the company.

Simple Interest - Simple interest is determined by multiplying the interest rate by the principal by the number of periods.

Solvency - The ability of a company to meet its long-term financial obligations.

Standard & Poor's 500 Index - S&P 500 – An index of 500 stocks designed as a leading indicator to reflect the risk and return characteristics of large cap companies.

Subprime - A categorization of borrowers with a poor credit history.

Tangible Asset - Assets that have a physical form or substance.

Tax Break – A tax savings received through deductions, credits and exemptions.

Tax Free – Referring to goods and services that are not taxed.

Trademark – A legal distinction through the use of a symbol, word, phrase or logo.

Treasury Bill - T-Bill - A U.S. government security sold in denominations of $1000 but at a discount with a maturity of less than one year.

Unsecured Loan – A loan based on a borrower's creditworthiness and not collateral.

Usury – The act of lending money at an unusually high interest rate.

Value Added – An improvement given to a product to differentiate and give it a higher sense of value.

Variable Interest Rate – An interest rate that changes or fluctuates over time.

Wealth – Having a large amount or abundance of valuable products or contents with an economical value that can be measured in price.

Financial Strengthening Workbook
3 Easy Steps to Financial Stability With Stress Free Budgeting
Includes Workbook and CD

An intensive work study to empower and motivate you to get control of your finances. You will learn to use budgeting as a vehicle for achieving your dreams and desires. This work study will coach the student through 3 easy steps, making budgeting less stress full and less time consuming.

To place your order, contact us at (302) 669-9156